DID YOU DO YOUR HOMEWORK? IS NOT ENOUGH!

Seven Motivating Principles for the Comprehensive Success of Parents and Their Children

By

AARON BRAXTON

This book is a work of fiction. Places, events, and situations in this story are purely fictional. Any resemblance to actual persons, living or dead, is coincidental.

© 2002 by Aaron Braxton. All rights reserved.

No part of this book may be reproduced, stored in a retrieval system, or transmitted by any means, electronic, mechanical, photocopying, recording, or otherwise, without written permission from the author.

ISBN: 1-4033-1443-8 (e-book)
ISBN: 1-4033-1444-6 (Paperback)

This book is printed on acid free paper.

1stBooks - rev. 4/21/03

Acknowledgments

I am a true believer that if you are trying to do positive, uplifting work, positive, uplifting energy will follow you. I've had the good fortune to meet some positive, spiritual, and enlightening people who have encouraged me tremendously in my quest to publish my ideas. First, and foremost, I would like to acknowledge the God presence in my life. Without him, I would be like the walking dead, constantly searching for direction. With him, my life has purpose and meaning beyond what I see and hear, but also what I feel.

Sometimes in your life when you feel like you're trying, but nothing seems to work, God sends you an angel. That angel came to me in the form of Dr. Tim Miller.

I had just passed the California Basic Educational Skills Test (CBEST) and was eager to start with the Los Angeles Unified School District. The only problem was, there was a freeze on hiring. Slightly discouraged, I went to church to contemplate my next maneuver.

While at church (it's been my custom to speak to the person sitting to the left and right of me) I happened to strike up a conversation with Dr. Tim Miller. Not knowing he was a principal, I spoke with him about my plans of becoming an educator. To my surprise, he was the exact person I needed to help me on my quest to guiding some of the finest minds in California.

When I was in third grade, I learned to distinguish the words *principle* from *principal* by the ending of the word princi***pal***. ***"Pal"*** means friend. Dr. Tim Miller has been a friend, mentor, and constant source of motivation.

To my best friend Dwayne McHenry. My mother always told me, "You are who your friends are, so choose them wisely." I hope I have half the good in me that Dwayne has in him. He and his lovely wife Shaunte McHenry have allowed me to have an open dialogue with them regarding relationships between parents and their children. One of which is outlined in the book.

I remember when I was 10 years old, my Aunty Catherine sat down with me and discussed the prospect of starting my own business selling various cleaning products. Even though I never went into that lucrative business of the 70's, I did comprehend the essence of our conversation. Even then I was listening.

To Mrs. Marcia Haskins who was a great assistant principal and now an even greater principal. Her new teacher meetings provided an insight into the everyday educational experience of teachers and students. Her leadership, guidance, and "cannon ball energy" during my first years of teaching aided in my professional development. She was one who faithfully encouraged teachers to find their own style, and incorporate that into the educational standards. I think I have.

To Catrisa Booker and Stephanie Lawrence who took time from their busy schedules to help edit some of the ideas for my book. Thank you for your unselfish generosity and invaluable comments.

To Samuel Taylor, my former assistant, and friend. You always had something positive to say during *all* my many writing endeavors.

To Mrs. Deborah Gayle whom I've had the sheer pleasure of discussing some of the concepts and prospects of my book. She's always been a joy to talk to because of her abundant sagacity, everlasting wisdom and constant encouragement.

Finally to my mom, Mrs. Regina L. Jamison, who never faltered in her interminable belief that I could do all the things of my heart. Throughout my life she's given me "a lifetime supply of gasoline when I felt I was running on fumes."

If you would like information on workshops, lectures, or other programs by Aaron Braxton, or to order any books or tapes, please contact:

Talk of the Town Productions

P.O. Box 56412

Los Angeles, CA 90056

a.k.braxton@worldnet.att.net

CONTENTS

ACKNOWLEDGMENTS .... *iii*
INTRODUCTION .... *xiii*
1. *HOW TO STUDY* *1*
2. *DEVELOPING THE LEADER INSIDE YOUR CHILD.* *46*
3. *TEACHABLE MOMENTS* *62*
4. *CHANGE IS NECESSARY* *78*
5. *IMAGINATION* *108*
6. *WHAT YOU OWE* *122*
7. *THE JOURNEY* *148*
INDEX *159*

INTRODUCTION

Gangs, teenage pregnancy, illiteracy, drugs, neglect, deviant behaviors, emotional and physical abuse, all contribute to poor self-esteem and a low emotional balance in children. Every day more and more parents are losing their children, not from a lack of love, but from a lack of know how. Parents are simply not aware of the simple things that will inspire their children to be better students, as well as better human beings. How many parents have ever used principles that required them to look within their own circumstances in order to find the answers they were desperately searching for in their children? This requires action.

Children respond to what you *say* and what you *do*. In order to create well balanced children, their emotional, physical, psychological, and spiritual beings must be in tact. Parents must be sensitive to this reality and work on achieving the best in themselves, so they can expect the best in their children.

Did You Do Your Homework? Is Not Enough! is an example of how to take a more dynamic role in the moral and educational development of children. It is packed with spirited principles, inspirational stories, and motivational techniques. Parents will learn that if they become more aware and open, there are many opportunities for them to teach, bond and relate to their children. This book shows parents how to develop relationships with their children that are healthy and mutually beneficial.

Did You Do Your Homework? Is Not Enough! is tailor made to fit each parent differently. That is the beauty of this book. It does not assume that every experience is the same, rather that every experience is individual, thus obtaining individualized results from universal themes. The theme that runs throughout this book is: you can do more for the well-being of your child by simply *doing more* and being open to change.

The first chapter of this book, **HOW TO STUDY**, deals with teaching children good study skills. Most parents expect that their children already know how to study, and most of them will say they know how as well. However, the truth of the matter is, most children have no idea what it takes to free their minds enough to be open and relaxed in order to retain information vital to their development. This chapter outlines a specific method that is easy, and most of all, practical. Topics covered in this chapter include: *Finding a Comfortable Place, Turning Off the Television, Turning Off the Radio, Organization, Time Management,* and *The Process of Studying*.

Chapter two shows how to **DEVELOP THE LEADER INSIDE *EVERY* CHILD.** These leadership principles vary from child to child and from situation to situation. The message is that every child has the innate ability to take charge of their own achievements. This chapter aids in achieving that capability. Topics covered in this chapter include: *Releasing Fear, Leadership Amongst Siblings,* and *Rebellion.*

The next three chapters are must do's for parents. These chapters include, **TEACHABLE MOMENTS, CHANGE IS NECESSARY,** and **IMAGINATION**. They re-enforce the fact that, in order to guide children in the right direction *you* must be headed in the *right* direction. It makes no sense to be headed down a one way street while you're trying to give someone directions. They take into account the notion that we must be responsible for our own actions and that we must hold ourselves to the highest standards. That if you're traveling down a one way street, you don't wait until you've hit someone to know that you have to change directions. After you've either seen the traffic sign or dodged a car, something should tell you to turn around and go the opposite direction before you hurt yourself and/or someone else.

Sometimes *change is necessary* in **you** in order for change to occur in your child. Sometimes there are *teachable moments* that, when realized, provide us with an opportunity for bonding and life long lessons. Sometimes we must build on our children's *imagination*.

There are too many distractions in the world that are producing virtual unimaginative children. It is vital that we build up their creativity. Children are a product of our society. They are our present as well as our future. Topics included in this chapter are: *The You In Them, You Are Not Your Child's Friend, Discipline, I Love You, Support, The Feeling Of Freedom, Don't Let the Small Stuff Get Ya!, Small Steps First, Mental Pictures, Silence,* and *Problem Solving.*

The last two chapters deal with **WHAT YOU OWE** as a parent and taking pleasure in **THE JOURNEY** you've made the choice to embark. Remember your children did not wake you one morning and say, "I think I'll be conceived today." It was your choice. Therefore, you *owe* them a happy and productive life. You also *owe* yourself pleasure in the *journey*. Topics in these chapters include: **Building Self Esteem, Money, Credit, Charity, Social Events, Religion, Humor, Mistakes,** and **Peace.**

Before you say, "Oh no! Not another textbook!" This is not a text book nor is it the traditional parenting book. The most important aspects of this book are, leisurely reading, common sense, and motivation. I wanted the principles to be easily understood without having a Ph.D. behind your name.

My goal is to give parents principles that will aid in their lives, thus aiding in the lives of their children. It's important. Our children are at stake and it is our responsibility as educators, parents and as a community to look after the best interest of them.

It is my sincere desire that you will receive what I was divinely inspired to write. It is my hope that you will apply these principles to your life and the lives of your children. It is my wish that you will find enrichment, inspiration, and success from every word, on every page I have written. God Bless.

Did You Do Your Homework? Is Not Enough!

1

HOW TO STUDY

HOW TO STUDY

If you ask most students do they know how to study, they will bluntly tell you, "Yes, of course!" They will say it with such a straight face that you will believe every word they say, and feel a little stupid for even asking the question in the first place. They will be so sincere in their answer that you will not even question them again. Why should you? They are in school, right? Isn't that where they are suppose to learn this indispensable technique?

Well, the truth is, that with large class sizes and dwindling educational funds many teachers find it difficult to teach children specific techniques on how to learn. It becomes the parent's responsibility to sit with their children and develop palpable methods in order to make it easier for their children to love to learn.

As a Teacher, it frustrated me that I would spend hours preparing lesson plans that I thought were interesting, educational, and fun, only to find that when I asked students to regurgitate information in the form of a test, many students failed. What I realized was that although students enjoyed my wonderful personality and teaching skills, when the period was over, their brains shut down. They had not been taught how to successfully retain information so that it could be useful at a later date (a la test time). That is what led me to develop a study skills technique which I taught to all my classes at the beginning of every school year. I was not going to let them have any more excuses to fail in my class, other classes, or in life. You know what? My students started doing well. This technique is easy, it can be taught at any age, and it's something that you and your child can do at home. Here is my technique:

FINDING A COMFORTABLE PLACE.

A *comfortable place* is anywhere that is cozy and has very few distractions. Bedroom, den, living room, kitchen table, even the bathroom, are all examples of comfortable places. Now, I know some people might be thinking, "The bathroom? This guy has lost his mind!" But like I say to my students, "Why do you think people take newspapers, magazines, or books into the bathroom? Because they're going to be in there for a while." It's a part of life and you might as well *kill two birds with one stone.* Other places might include the library (if close to home) or a park (only if it's safe).

One of the areas most children, as well as adults, like to study is on the bed. When asked, most children will swear that they've never had a problem studying on their beds. My notion is, just like many dreams are forgotten, so are many people's memories.

NEVER STUDY ON THE BED!

Your bed is the only place designated *too comfortable.* It is a place of rest, total relaxation and most definitely, sleep. Once on your bed, your body involuntarily says that it is time to snooze. You may have the best intentions in the world, but your body will have another agenda entirely.

What most students say is that it doesn't happen to them. What *I* say is that it happens to just about everyone. How many times have you tried to study in bed only to wake up the next morning laying on crumpled papers? (All of your books have been scattered all over the bedroom, so that you could get more comfortable as you slept.) Every good intention went out the window when your cells started shutting down one by one in order for your body to get ready for sleep. That's because your body felt that since you were on your bed, it must be time to sleep. You have no control over this act, it's totally involuntary.

I like to create the picture of a piping hot pizza with pepperoni, Italian sausage, green bell peppers, and mushrooms into the heads of my students. Before I can even finish, they're telling me that I'm making them hungry. Then I tell them to feel their heart or get connected to the blinking of their eyes. By this time they're looking at me completely crazy.

What we don't realize is there are some things that are completely uncontrollable. Just like you can not control the fact that you get hungry, the beating of your heart, or the blinking of your eyes, you also can not control whether you will fall asleep when studying on your bed. You will! It's uncontrollable, inevitable, involuntary, and it happens to the best of us.

TURN OFF THE TELEVISION

Turning off the television is one your child will fight you tooth and nail. They will tell you that it's easier to study with the TV playing. They have been conditioned to think that they need activity going in order for them to function properly. The scenario goes something like this:

Student comes home from school. With the best intentions in the world, student lays all materials

Did You Do Your Homework? Is Not Enough!

needed to study out around the table. He is ready, but it's 5 o'clock, and all the syndicated shows start coming on. Your child can't resist the temptation. He tells himself that if it's a show that he's seen before he'll turn it off. He waste ten minutes looking for the remote. When he finally locates it, he turns to his favorite syndicated show. Of course it's one he's seen before. But this episode is a good one. It's reallllllllllly funny and he convinces himself that after it's over he'll turn off the television and get back to studying. But what usually happens? There's a commercial that previews the next syndicated show and your child, yet again, convinces himself that after *that* one is over he'll start studying. But again, what happens? There's another preview for the next show and your child comes up with the next brilliant idea. He'll do his homework between the commercials!

So your child starts watching the next syndicated show. The commercials come on and your child rushes to start his homework. Now, commercials are only between 30 seconds and 1 minute long and usually there are about 2 to 3 that run at a time. That means your child has approximately two minutes to scratch out something that looks like work. That's what he does. He quickly starts scratching out the work. He's not paying attention to neatness, grammar or structure. All he's thinking about is

Did You Do Your Homework? Is Not Enough!

getting that particular section done before the commercial is over. He does, and he's particularly proud of himself having accomplished that small feat. He really thinks he's *killing two birds with one stone.* The show comes back on and he can relax feeling that his work is getting done. The next commercial comes on and again your child rushes to do his work. Again, he's not paying attention to what he's doing, he just wants to get the work done. The commercial goes off, and again your child can watch his TV show relaxing comfortably on a job he *thinks* is well done. What tends to happen by the next commercial is that your child gets sucked into commercial land.

Aaron Braxton

Commercials by their very nature are designed to draw you into them. They are created to sell a product and the more interesting and creative they can be, the better. That is why four hours later your child will get up from the trance of television with only a fraction of his work done. All the good intentions in the world won't erase the fact that his teacher will be asking for his work and he will bring every excuse dating back to when my grandparents were students as to the why it's not completed. How can you get around this scenario? **TURN OFF THE TV!**

Did You Do Your Homework? Is Not Enough!

TURN OFF ALL MUSIC

This is another area that children will fight you like cats and dogs over. They will say that while most kids may not be able to listen to their favorite CD or the radio, they are the exception. Don't believe them.

Studying takes concentration. How can you expect your child to concentrate when part of their brain is listening to the words of their favorite songs? Even if the music is turned down low, part of their brain is listening for "that song" and when it comes on effective studying is lost forever. The reason being is that part of the brain will always be listening out for the next "song." However, having said that, there is one exception: instrumental jazz or instrumental classical music.

Research has shown that instrumental jazz and instrumental classical music may improve children's thinking patterns. I tried it with my own students and it worked! At first they fought me as if their life depended on it. They said they absolutely hated jazz and classical music. They felt the music was boring and tiring. They wanted me to play more upbeat vocal music; the type of music that might be heard on MTV, VH1 or BET. Then I explained to them that they actually listened to jazz or classical music just about every day. Of course they didn't believe me until I pointed out such movies as "Titanic,"

Did You Do Your Homework? Is Not Enough!

which features a host of classical music, and the television show "The Simpsons," which features jazz. I pointed out to them that virtually every movie, television, or commercial is scored by using classical or jazz music.

It's always nice when children are able to see the practicality of things. It's even better when it's shown on their level in a way that best fits their needs. After I pointed out that they had not only listened to classical and jazz music, but in fact had *enjoyed* it, they could not get enough of it. Even on days when I did not turn on the radio, they would ask me if they could turn it to the classical or jazz stations.

Remember, **TURN OFF ALL MUSIC**. The only exception would be to softly play classical or jazz. Given the choice, most kids will opt to keep the stereo off. If they choose to listen to classical or jazz, then hey, the research can't be all that bad.

ORGANIZATION

Most students have a real problem with the concept of organization. They have no clue as to what it means to be organized and how it relates to their success.

Most students think that being organized means carrying their backpacks to school everyday with a bunch of crumpled up papers and *maybe* a pencil or pen. However, there is something called *maximized time* and it is useful because it relies on the notion that what you put into it, you will get out of it ten fold. It means that you take the extra time to get organized now, and you save time in the long run.

Organization starts at the beginning of the year. It begins when you go out and buy supplies for your child's first day of school. You want to buy supplies that are practical and useful. You also want to begin this process with your child present. It is important that children understand the proper tools that will aid them on the road to being a successful student. You would think this is common sense stuff, but you'd be surprised some of the supplies or *lack* of supplies children bring to class.

How many times have you looked through your child's backpack only to find jumbled, crumpled up papers scattered throughout every nook and cranny? Once you locate their notebook through the snarled mess, you may find math work in the English section and social studies work in the science section. Here's a way that will quickly and effecttively get your child in better shape so he will be on his way to becoming a better organized student.

Start with a large three ring binder with at least 300 sheets of paper. Again, this is something that

Did You Do Your Homework? Is Not Enough!

must be done *with* your child so that it can be duplicated year after year. You want the binder large enough so that it can incorporate several classes. Make sure the notebook has dividers so that every subject can be separated by periods. You want 1st period in the front, 2nd period next, and so on. If the notebook does not have dividers, they can be easily made with a little tape and paper. They can also be purchased at the school student store. Different colored construction paper works great as well.

Within each subject divider your child places 30 sheets of paper. If it's elementary school, then it would be the entire 300 sheets of paper. The rest of the paper goes to the *back* of the notebook. This is the paper that will be used for the restocking of each subject. Once a particular subject has been depleted, then fill that subject with the paper from the back of the notebook. Most students when they have exhausted one subject's paper, will automatically pull from other subjects. This manner creates disorganization.

Some schools offer student planners at the beginning of every school year. These planners are great for developing organizational skills. Inside is valuable information about school rules and expectations, as well as, helpful hints on becoming excellent students. Within every planner is also a calendar which has the four academic subjects printed inside for every school day. Students are able to write down when an assignment was given, and *more importantly* when it is due.

If your child's school does not offer free student planners, then you can purchase one as part of your child's supplies or you can have him or her write out their assignments on a small notepad. Never have them rely on writing their assignments in the subject part of their notebooks for two reasons: one, you want to be able to easily check that they are completing their assignments; two, they forget. It's that simple. They will undoubtedly forget because they will not check their notebooks. They must have something separate that they know they must check everyday in order to become a better organized and systematized student.

TIME MANAGEMENT

Time plays a very important role in the success or failure of your child. It is also a factor that is often over looked or devalued by parents as well as students.

When it comes to studying, students need to be set on a schedule. When you think about it, it makes sense. We put babies on a schedule when they are infants so mothers will be able to get needed rest. As responsible adults, we are on various schedules from when we wake each morning, to when we have to be at work, to when we pay taxes, to when we go to bed at night. It is no different for children.

Enforcing a study schedule onto your child can be difficult if one is not already in place. However, just as it was difficult at first to put your infant on a schedule, it was necessary and extremely helpful. Children need structure and this is one way to give it to them in a stable environment in which they will achieve academically.

Structure also means that they must study at the same time everyday with as few exceptions as possible. This process puts their brains in a sort of ready mode. It gives the brain an opportunity to prepare for what it needs to receive, in order for the mind to be successful. To better illustrate my point I always resort back to the example of the involuntary actions of your body.

At around 12 o'clock P.M. just about every child in America starts to get hungry. Why? Because we have placed them on a schedule that says *that's* when they are suppose to eat lunch. So, at around noon their brains start sending signals to their stomachs that their bodies are hungry. How does the body respond? It responds by clearing the stomach and making room for the coming nutrients (or in many cases, junk).

Did You Do Your Homework? Is Not Enough!

That's the same concept when dealing with studying at the same time everyday. You want your child's mind to get used to a time schedule. In that way, when it comes time to study, the brain will begin to prepare the mind to retain the needed information your child puts into it. The next question then becomes, "When is a good time to study?"

Most Parents want their children to study right when they get home from school. How many times have you heard your own parents yelling, "Do your homework!" right when you walked through the door. Although it may be the most convenient time to study, it's certainly not the best time.

Aaron Braxton

The best time to begin studying in order to give your brain an optimum workout is at least 1 hour after school or 1 hour after dinner. The reason being, when students first get home from school they are tired. They've just had six or six and one half hours of continuous brain activity. They need a chance to relax and unwind. This is the time they can get a snack, take a nap, or talk on the phone. (Keep them away from the TV or stereo for the reasons mentioned earlier.) Only after they've been home for an hour do they need to begin the process of studying. This way their bodies have a chance to recline and their brain's have a chance to prepare.

Did You Do Your Homework? Is Not Enough!

If an hour after school does not work for your particular time restraints, then try an hour after dinner. You never want to force your child to study right after dinner because, again, they will be tired. Remember the involuntary actions of your body. After one eats, the body tells itself it needs to digest the food. The best way to aid in digestion is to be still. This comes in the form of sleep. How many times have you eaten a nice dinner and went to relax on the couch only to find that you've dozed off for a few hours? That's because your body needs rest in order to properly digest its food. For that reason alone it is best to wait at least an hour after your child has eaten to begin the process of studying.

This way your child is alert and ready to retain the much needed information required for his or her academic success.

THE PROCESS OF STUDYING

Okay, your child has found a comfortable place to study. You've turned off the TV and the stereo. Your child's notebook is organized by subject matter and you've established the best *time* to begin studying. Now, do you just tell your child to, "*Get to it*"? Of course not! There is a specific technique to the actual process of studying.

Most children do their homework without any regard to the fact that they are actually studying. They just want to complete it as quickly as possible

Did You Do Your Homework? Is Not Enough!

so they can go on with what they think is their life. The majority don't care about the most important factor in doing homework. That is retention.

Teachers give homework because it aids in what was done in the classroom. It also aids in the retention of such work so teachers may build on that work from the previous day. If students don't pay particular attention to their homework, or simply don't do it, there's a good chance they will fall behind in that particular subject area. For example, let's say a teacher has given a lesson on sentence structure. The first day the lesson plan dealt with how to write a complete sentence using a subject and predicate. After providing a detailed explanation to the class, and giving class work to supplement the discussion, the teacher assigns homework. For whatever the reason your child decides not to do it and comes back to class with an incomplete assignment.

As the teacher, I expect everyone to finish the assignment. Therefore, the next day I would build on what they have already learned and introduce compound sentences. Again, I assign homework to supplement what they were to have already learned. Again, your child does not understand because while the rest of the class was doing the class assignment, I was trying to explain the previous day's homework assignment to your child before

Did You Do Your Homework? Is Not Enough!

the end of the period. Already your child is falling behind and it can happen just that quickly.

A more long term example would be if your child hasn't committed his multiplication tables to memory by the 3rd grade. It will get very difficult for him as he moves up in grades. For example, he gets to 6th grade and still doesn't have them mastered. He is definitely going to fall behind because his teacher is going to expect a certain skill level he doesn't have, because he did not take the time to do his homework.

The process of studying doesn't mean just "doing" your homework. It means dissecting information, keeping in mind that the information is or will be useful **now** and/or in the **future**. This specific technique incorporates reading all *introductions, headings, questioning, silent reading, narrating* and *reviewing*.

READING INTRODUCTIONS

Most students, whether they are beginning to read a textbook or novel, will automatically skip over the *Introductions*. They feel that it is a waste of their valuable time to read what they feel is often boring and unnecessary. They would rather get right into the story of a novel or the text of a textbook. I say students must read **everything** including the *Introductions*.

Did You Do Your Homework? Is Not Enough!

Introductions are a very important part of textbooks and novels. They usually give essential information concerning what it is you are about to read. They are fundamental in preparing your brain for the task ahead. Therefore if they are skipped, one's brain is constantly playing "catch up." The brain then begins the task of trying to figure out "what's going on." However, if you had read the *introductions* you would have found out that the author had conveniently previewed each chapter ahead of time.

HEADINGS

Headings are all the bold typed titles in textbooks. They must be read **after** you have read the *Introduction* and **before** you begin reading the text. They are important because they tell the brain the subject matter it is about to study. Utilizing all headings allows the student an opportunity to create questions ahead of time regarding the particular subject matter to be read.

QUESTIONING

Creating questions is an important tool in the studying process. Students must create questions from the headings. For example, a student is

Did You Do Your Homework? Is Not Enough!

studying from his English textbook. The subject he or she is studying is "The Sentence." Some of the *headings* may read **"Kinds of Sentences"**, **"Classifying Sentences"**, and **"Subject and Predicates."** From these previewed headings the student should be able to come up with a few questions based from them. Let's look at the heading titled, **"Kinds of Sentences."**

There are several questions that a student could come up with regarding **"Kinds of Sentences."** Some questions may include; "What is a sentence?" "How many kinds of sentences are there?" "Are there different purposes for each different kind of sentence?"

"**Classifying Sentences**", and "**Subject and Predicates**", are also headings that a student should be able to apply questions. For example, a question may be "How do I classify sentences?," or "What is the difference between a subject and a predicate?" These are all questions that must be asked *before* the student starts to actually read the text. The reason is that you want the student's brain to be actively seeking out the answers to the questions as he or she is reading the information.

This technique also applies to any questions that might be at the back of the section the student is reading. The student must read those questions *first* as well. Again, you want your brain to be actively

Did You Do Your Homework? Is Not Enough!

seeking out the information *as* it is reading. This will make it easier for the student to retain information needed to do his or her work. Another point that must be made is that the same technique also applies to *test taking*.

When one is taking a test, one should always survey the questions first. Particularly when the test involves some type of reading comprehension. The student should always read the questions first, then read the paragraphs. Many times the student may not have to even read the entire paragraphs before answering all the questions. The bottom line, **read all Headings FIRST.**

Aaron Braxton

SILENT READING

Silent reading entails reading the information or text to your yourself. It involves allowing your brain to process information in a quiet, serene manner. Most students want to speed read through this process. However, that does not work. What must be done is just the opposite. Students need to slow down their reading process. In this way they are able to retain much more information because their concentration level is higher. They are also able to find the answers to the questions they developed because they've slowed down their thought process. This allows the brain an opportunity to sift through information casually and efficiently.

NARRATING

Narrating means to verbally answer all questions aloud without looking at the text. This includes the questions that students think of themselves, as well as any questions at the end of a particular section, or any questions that may be assigned as homework.

When I introduce this section to my class, most students are kind of leery at first. They don't trust that this exercise is for their benefit. Most suggest that I'm trying to make them look crazy in front of their parents, siblings, or friends. Nonetheless, this exercise is important for a couple of reasons.

The first reason is that students need to process information through their brains as many times as possible. By *narrating* information aloud, the brain is not only processing information by *sight*, it is also processing information by *ear*. This means that the brain is also listening to what the voice says, thus information is sifting through the brain an extra time. Remember, you want information to be processed through the brain in as little time as possible, with as little effort as possible.

The second reason is that a child who is able to listen to their own voice begins to develop their own sense of learning style. How many times have we read something silently and not fully understood it's

Did You Do Your Homework? Is Not Enough!

meaning until we read it aloud? There's something about reading aloud, that gives the brain an extra opportunity to comprehend information. How many times have you used the phrase, "That doesn't sound right?" Reciting aloud instantly tells you what you know, what you don't know, what you've learned and what you need to learn.

By *narrating* aloud students begin to test their critical thinking skills on themselves. They become better thinkers and more confident speakers. They also gain the ability to make use of the phrase, *"That doesn't sound right!,"* more effectively.

REVIEWING

Reviewing is the process of going back over everything that the student has studied thus far. I know students will want to skip this step deeming it unnecessary. However, it plays an essential role in the study development method.

If the student has done the previous steps effectively, this process should only take a few minutes. It involves going back over the *headings*, *questioning*, and *narrating* sections. Keep in mind that the *reviewing* process is all done aloud. This way the student is instantly able to figure out what he or she has learned and what he or she has not learned.

Did You Do Your Homework? Is Not Enough!

If I go through the reviewing steps of reading the headings (it reminds me what I've studied), asking myself questions (it tells me what I've learned) and I still do not understand something, I do not have to go back over the entire subject matter. I only have to review what I have not learned or do not completely understand. If after the review process, I still don't understand, then I'll have a viable question to ask either my parents or my teacher the following day. In this way the learning process is always constant. When a student ask a parent or teacher about something he or she did not quite understand, but gave considerable thought, it makes the learning process easier. Once an explanation is given the brain is able to connect the dots because it has thought about the puzzle.

The steps to studying outlined in this chapter are masterful ways to involve your child in the joys of learning. It may be a lot different from what your child is used to, but it still is important. It may be time consuming at first, but like anything else, once your child gets the hang of it he or she will be done in no time. One must always keep in mind that there is virtually no profession that does not require some sort of studying (and if there is I don't think you want your child to be a part of it). We, as responsible human beings will be studying till the day we make our transition from this earth. Why not

Did You Do Your Homework? Is Not Enough!

develop an effective way that one can start as early as possible, and carry with them throughout their journey through this amazing process called, *life*?

2

Developing the *Leader* *Inside* Your Child

DEVELOPING THE LEADER INSIDE YOUR CHILD.

What is a *Leader?* Most people would characterize a leader as someone who is has the ability to get things done. Others may say that a leader is someone who people follow. I say a leader has all those qualities and more. The greatest attribute a leader can possess is the ability to think positively for himself and influence others to do the same.

As a parent raising a child in the new millennium you want your child to be able to think for himself for a variety of reasons. There are so many situations your child may become involved in that they need to possess the ability to analyze situations quickly and safely. They need to fearlessly question themselves by asking; "How is this situation going to effect my life positively so that I may affect others?"

Now you may think, "Hey this is just a bit heavy for my 10 year old child. He is nobody's leader. He's just trying to get through the 5th grade!" What I would say is that your child possesses all the qualities in him to be a leader in the classroom and in life.

Have you ever been in a classroom where the teacher has no control of the class? Usually it's one or two students who are ruining the learning experience of the majority. If your child were a part of that classroom, which would you want your child to be, the ringleader or the class follower?

As a teacher, I focus my attention on the ringleader because I know I can re-enforce his negative

Did You Do Your Homework? Is Not Enough!

behavior with positive behavior modification. Being a ringleader tells me that the student has natural leadership abilities. It tells me the student is energetic, and a lot of times, extremely witty. If I can plug into that essence I can alter the behavior from negative to positive. Usually the rest of the class will follow suit. However, what about the *rest of the class*?

Even within the class followers, there are leaders who just haven't been taught how to *be* leaders. It is your role as a parent to instill these qualities in your child before they start school. By the time they reach the classroom, teachers should not have to spend 75% of their time on discipline and 25% on instruction. Your child should come to class with the basic structure of how to be great students and even better leaders.

Here's the perfect opportunity to recognize leadership qualities in your child. Re-enforce negative behavior with positive behavior, and if your child exhibits follower characteristics, turn them into leadership attributes.

RELEASING FEAR

Fear is something that plagues all of us. It stifles many people. It is especially prevalent in school age children. I've had the opportunity to listen to children talk with each other and I've been surprised

Did You Do Your Homework? Is Not Enough!

at some of the names they call each other. One of the names that I was most shocked by was the term "schoolboy/schoolgirl."

To be a schoolboy or schoolgirl is to be a student that does his or her homework, studies hard, and get good grades in school. Somehow children have taken this trait to mean something negative. They will call anyone whom they feel "studies too much" this name. It is malicious in manner and often very hurtful to the targeted student.

The afflicted student feels alienated and often, inadequate. That student will then go through great lengths to appear moronic. Many times it is *that* student who is disruptive and often disrespectful.

Other times the afflicted student can appear silent and uninvolved. In both cases *fear* is what is holding that student back from becoming all that he or she can be.

Fear means: *f*alse *e*nergy *a*ppearing *r*eal. It is a very powerful emotion. It must be taught to overcome at the school age level or it will lead to many problems later in life. What would happen if that student who was being called "schoolboy or schoolgirl" was actually told that it was his or her **right** to be smart? How do you think that little phrase would change his or her perspective on how they feel about themselves?

Did You Do Your Homework? Is Not Enough!

I once had a student named Eduardo. He was handsome, rambunctious, athletic, and extremely academically gifted. Unfortunately, Eduardo didn't mind glorifying all of this attributes *except* for the one that dealt with his brain. He wanted people to think that he was just an average kid. As a result, any test he scored an A+, he would tuck neatly away in his backpack. He never wanted any of the other students to know his grades or how truly academically gifted he was. He didn't want to be called a "schoolboy". It wasn't until the end of the semester when the final points were posted on the wall of the classroom that anyone knew that

Eduardo received the highest total points. He was furious, but I was proud.

I explained to Eduardo that there was nothing wrong or abnormal about being a schoolboy. It was his **right** to be smart and he had a **right** to reap whatever benefits or rewards that came with hard work. It meant that he was being everything he was suppose to be.

An amazing transformation happened in Eduardo and the class that following second semester. He was still his rambunctious self, but he had started to take pride in his written assignments. Whenever he would receive the highest grade out of my entire class, he would say aloud, "It's because I'm smart!"

Did You Do Your Homework? Is Not Enough!

He walked a little taller, his chest poked out a little farther, and he felt better about his total person. He was beginning to see himself as he should be. That not only changed his perspective, but it changed the perspective of the class as well.

Once the class saw the newfound Eduardo, they started to take more pride in their work as well. It was as if Eduardo had unconsciously given them permission. With his words and his deeds Eduardo had become a fully actualized leader and the class began the task of leading for themselves.

Aaron Braxton

LEADERHIP AMONGST SIBLINGS

When there are multiple children in your family there is always one child who positions himself as the leader of the other siblings. Most parents will ignore this fact and either try and raise their children the same or try and raise them individually. Both ways can be tiring and taxing to the body and spirit.

We live in an age where time becomes a definite factor. There are many single parent households and if there are two parent households, usually both parents work. Even if there are only two siblings, it can get tiresome trying to individualize your teachings.

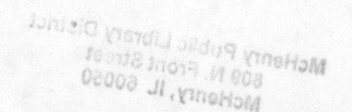

Did You Do Your Homework? Is Not Enough!

It is the parent's obligation and responsibility to recognize leadership abilities in their children while they are *young*: especially that child who leads the rest of the siblings. Parents must re-enforce positive behavior in that child and that child will influence the rest of the siblings. Other siblings will listen to that child as long as they feel they are being treated fairly. This frees you as the parent to become more involved with your children.

Once the other children begin to mimic the behavior of the leader child you can focus your attention on observing them individually. This is because they will have received behavioral fundamentals from the leader child. It now becomes easier to deal with their different personalities. However, if you try to begin by teaching your children as a whole, you will be so overworked that nothing will get done and your children end up lost in the process.

How many times have we seen, known, or read about entire siblings who were underachievers? In many cases it's not because their parents were bad people. It's because they didn't understand how to focus their attention on their children when their children were younger. As a result nothing was accomplished and as their children grew older it became harder and harder to deal with them. On the other hand, what about the family who's siblings are all high achievers? What are some of the reasons why this takes place?

In most families where the siblings are high achievers, there was a great focus on the leader child. This child, in turn, taught the other siblings either by deed or by example. Johnny, age 6, began reading so Adam, age 3, who wanted to be like his older brother began to pick up books and mimic him. In this manner the parents didn't have to spend the time convincing Adam to read. He eagerly did that from watching his leader brother. This way the parent or parents could spend quality time developing proper reading skills and not spending unnecessary time trying to convince Adam to read.

There's also more time to get to know their children's individual personalities. This will be helpful when deciding reading material that fits each siblings personality and thus making the process more enjoyable for parent and child.

REBELLION

There may be times when siblings rebel. In these cases they may view the leader child as a "suck-up." Many times they may even cause problems in the household. In those cases there are a few options. You may want to reevaluate your choice for the leader child. Maybe your choice for the leader child was not the best choice. (In most cases the leader

Did You Do Your Homework? Is Not Enough!

child is the oldest child, *but not always.*) Maybe you choice was correct, but you didn't deal with the other siblings' unique personalities. In this case, you may have inadvertently lumped the other siblings together. It is very important that you focus on the other children individually and not as a whole.

Also remember, your children are "getting it." If you've done your part in instilling good leadership qualities in your leader child, the other siblings see it. They may not always agree, but they get it. Constantly build on their personalities and the rest will follow.

3

*Teachable **Moments***

TEACHABLE MOMENTS

There are always these *little moments* that parents or teachers get that are perfect opportunities for us to connect and teach children. The trick is to be open and aware that they exist. You must seize each moment, because once it's lost, you can't get it back. There are three stories that come to mind

Did You Do Your Homework? Is Not Enough!

about *teachable moments* that were lost or found. All involve parents that are great providers, loving souls, and wonderful human beings.

MYCHAEL AND AMBER

I was having dinner with my friend Mychael and he informed me that he and Amber, age 10, had gone into a book store in order to search for a particular book he wanted to read. While searching the aisles for the book, Amber wandered off into the section of books that were authored by motivational speakers. While browsing through some of the books, she came across a book by a well known female spiritual motivational speaker. After investing considerable time in reading the first few pages, the book engaged her enough for her to ask her dad to buy it for her. Without even thinking about it, Mychael said, "No."

Of course my first question was, "Why?" His response was that he felt the book was "too grown up" and that some of the concepts discussed by the writer would be "over Amber's head."

My response was, "So what!" Many of the ideas discussed in the book very well may be over the head of Amber, but this particular author discussed how people could live their lives successfully and spiritually. That's a concept I would have loved to have embraced at age 10!

Did You Do Your Homework? Is Not Enough!

This father was not being a "bad" father. It's not that he didn't want his child to read, in fact he sent her off to the children's section for that purpose. He was doing what he thought was the right thing for his child. Mychael never intended to discourage Amber. He was trying to spare her the difficulty of decoding big word and trying to understand complex sentences and ideas. He simply felt he had Amber's best interest in heart and mind. But what about those big words, complex sentences, and philosophical ideas that all discuss successful ways of life Amber may not understand at ten years old?

First, you never want to discourage children from reading something that could possibly enrich their lives. Second, Amber **wanted** to read the book. It didn't have any profanity, nudity or vulgarity. Third, suppose Amber didn't comprehend the majority of the book? So what! Even if she received one concept from the entire book, she would have learned more than she knew previously. The reward comes from the attempt. Also, if you want to grow academically, you must always attempt things that are above your head. Otherwise you grow stagnant. In this case, the book did have philosophical *life* concepts, and here is where the *teachable moments* evolve.

Suppose Amber read a particular concept in the book that she did not understand. Who do you think

Did You Do Your Homework? Is Not Enough!

she would have gone to for explanation? This could have created a *teachable moment* in which father and daughter could have bonded. He could have broken down the concepts into ideas that she could understand. Thus, it could have turned into a moment in which he could have yielded her life some direction at a time when she was *most* receptive. Maybe *he* could have read the book to her. Maybe *they* could have read the book *jointly,* creating their own private book club. That would have given them nice moments where they could have discussed the ideas in the book together—bonding moments.

Nevertheless that moment in time was lost and can never be recaptured. Although there will be other *teachable moments,* time is something you must not waste. You must always stay connected and be aware that these moments exist. And you must be ready, willing, and able to respond the moment they arise.

As a teacher, I have sometimes underestimated my students. In the case of Mychael, it is quite possible he could have underestimated Amber. He had a preconceived notion about his child that may or may not have been right. The trouble is, for that moment, he'll never know.

Did You Do Your Homework? Is Not Enough!

TANEISHA AND AVERY JACKSON

One afternoon in my 5th period class I was checking students homework. As I approached Avery, I asked him had he completed his homework assignment. Without looking at me, his response was, "No," and he quickly handed me a note from his mom. The note read "Avery did not understand the homework. Please call me."

Later that evening after I'd had dinner and settled down a bit, I decided to give Mrs. Jackson a call. When she answered the phone she told me that she was very concerned about the fact that her son did not understand the homework. She wanted to make it very clear that she wasn't blaming me, but that she wanted to teach her son a lesson. My immediate question was, "What lesson did you want to teach him?" She responded angrily by stating that she felt her son was lazy, and that he needed to ask questions when he did not understand something. My response to her was that, "Yes he may not have understood something, but that doesn't necessarily mean he was lazy in his attempt. In fact, he may have understood the assignment in class, but forgot how to do it when he got home." That's perfectly normal. It happens to everyone, including adults.

The moment Avery went to his mother and asked for her help on an assignment, it became a *teachable moment*. This was a moment when mother and son

Did You Do Your Homework? Is Not Enough!

could have discussed the reason or reasons *why* Avery did not understand the assignment. If she had probed him a bit she would have discovered that it wasn't that he was lazy, but that he felt insecure. Shaming him was not going to help that individual situation. He needed to be nurtured. He needed to be assured that he could come to his mom for any clarification he may need regarding his assignments. He needed to feel confident that his mom did not judge him in a negative light. He needed support not ridicule.

The *teachable moment* would have arisen had Mrs. Jackson sat down with her son and given him every thing he needed (aside from doing the assignment herself) to possess a completed assignment. Afterwards, they could have discussed the reasoning behind why Avery was too afraid to ask for clarification or extra help. She may have suggested ways in which he could have approached his teacher in a manner that would be most successful for him. It may be that Avery could have approached his teacher after class. Maybe after school. Maybe his teacher could have called him at home. Maybe this could have lead to a discussion about the importance of *self*. Mrs. Jackson could have discussed with Avery the mere fact that no one in his class knows everything. That's why they're in this magnificent place called school and he is there to learn like everyone else. It could have been explained in such a way that would have empowered him. That way he would have felt a little more comfortable about getting extra clarification. By sending Avery back to school with an incomplete assignment and a sense of confusion, set him back academically, even if for a day. It was a lost moment for Mrs. Jackson and especially a lost moment for Avery.

DON AND PAXTON MILLER

Don Miller lived with his three sons in area of town where they could not play in the front yard for fear of violence. He decided that he would save his money in order to move his family to an area where they all felt safe and revitalized. The "fruits of his labor" paid off, and within a year and a half he was able to purchase a spacious four bedroom home, with a large swimming pool and jacuzzi, in a quiet suburban neighborhood.

The weekend after they moved in and everything was settled, the three boys decided to go swimming. The day was extremely hot and two of the boys seemed to be having the time of their life splashing around in the deep end of the pool.

When Don came out to join his sons he noticed that his younger son Paxton was not enjoying himself in the pool like his two older brothers. He also noticed that Paxton kept to himself in the

Did You Do Your Homework? Is Not Enough!

shallow end of the pool. No matter what his brothers said, Paxton was not confident swimming into any level of water that was over his head. Don, knowing Paxton was a capable swimmer, asked him why he wasn't enjoying the full length of the pool. Paxton's response was that the water was too deep and he did not want to drown.

At that moment Don could have made the choice to say, "Okay, you swim to the other side of the pool when you're ready." However, recognizing that swimming in the deep end was something his son really wanted to do, he decided to seize the opportunity and capture the moment.

Don jumped into the shallow end of the pool and told his son to start at the shallow end, and continue to swim across the pool to the deep end. He assured his son that through his swim, he would never leave his side. Trusting his Dad, Paxton started the swim to the other side.

As Paxton neared the deeper parts of the pool, his body started to tire from fatigue. Knowing that his son might panic, Don gave him a little nudge to let Paxton know he was still beside him. It was all Paxton needed to reach the other side.

When Paxton touched the other end of the pool, he was so excited. His excitement not only elated

Did You Do Your Homework? Is Not Enough!

his dad, but his brothers as well. He kept shouting, "I made it! I made it!"

Don never mentioned the fact that it was him who helped his son reach the other end of the pool. His example showed Paxton that even through difficult times, he had a dad who would be there for him and share in his fears, as well as his victories, unselfishly.

4

Change *is* Necessary

CHANGE IS NECESSARY

A parent is a child's greatest example. You are their role model, they trust you, and they are watching your every move. When you have a parent conference, they are watching you. When you are at the grocery store, they are watching. When you are running late and there's a traffic jam on the freeway and you want to "go postal" on everyone in close proximity, they are still watching you. Even when you are gossiping on the phone, they are watching you. We sometimes forget that like a kitten who fiercely watches its mother in order to learn survival techniques, children acutely learn from their parents. If there are aspects of your life that are not productive, then it is *you* who needs to change for the sake of your children.

Change is a very difficult process. Many of us want to stay in the *familiar* instead of branching out into what is *unfamiliar*. That's where change lies. It's in the unknown: the uncomfortable; the discontent. Being content doesn't accomplish growth. Without growth there is stagnation. If you expect your child to grow, then you must continue to grow as well. That means you as a parent must act like the person you want your child to be. That means *change is necessary*.

THE <u>YOU</u> IN <u>THEM</u>

There are many ways parents must change in order to raise healthy academically successful children. One way is to have a clear vision for your life so that it resonates in the lives of your children. Take the story of **Regina**:

Regina was a 25 year old mother of two who because of physical and emotional abuse, found herself divorced, with no viable skills and only a high school education.

At 29 and living in a rodent infested two bedroom project apartment, Regina decided she needed to make a change in her life and the lives of her young children. Around this time of enlightenment, Regina's place of employment was offering an opportunity for anyone willing, to attend Boston University at the company's expense. Understanding the sacrifices would be great, but the rewards would be astronomical, Regina jumped at the opportunity. Knowing that she would not get home until late in the evening, she taught her eldest child how to warm up the food she had prepared.

She also checked every night to make sure their homework was complete as well as the house chores. Another important fact was that she checked with her neighbors to make sure her children stuck to their 6:00 P.M. curfew (utilizing the concept, "It takes an entire village to raise a child"). In the end, Regina graduated from Boston University, with honors.

As Regina's two children grew into early teens there was never a mention of the fact that they must go to college. She never said, "You will attend and graduate from college." It was expected. Her children remembered the late evening sounds of Motown along with the pitter patter of the typewriter on which she used to type all her class papers and projects. It was a comforting sound for them because they knew their mother was doing her very best. That memory was all that was needed to resonate in their mind, body, and spirit.

When it was time for both Regina's children to attend college she regrettably could not afford to financially support them. Times again became hard when she lost her job due to down sizing. With one child in college and the other about to attend, they could have given up and dropped out. However, the spirit is extremely pliable and memories are very strong. Both her children remembered the pitter patter of that electric typewriter and they said to themselves, if their mother could get through college raising two kids and working full-time, then they could get through college working part-time without any kids. Even when Regina did not know her children were watching her, they were watching her! They were taking mental notes and storing them in their brain's data banks to be retrieved at a later time when they would be needed for inspiration.

With encouraging letters, motivational cards, and heartening phone calls both Regina's children graduated from Universities. Money was tight, and there were times when both children wanted to quit,

Did You Do Your Homework? Is Not Enough!

but memories are strong and an encouraging word, or phrase from a parent goes a long way.

Regina's children became successful because *she* chose to be successful. This is not about finances, she gave her children a bigger gift than that. She gave them the gift of knowing they can *be, do,* and *go* anywhere they set their minds. She gave them freedom. And the story doesn't end there. Regina, seeing the strength in her children, decided to go back to school to get her Masters degree. She graduated with honors from the University of San Francisco. She now teaches and counsels students at a Junior College in Georgia. Change is necessary. Regina proved it in her life, the lives of her kids, and with the courage to grow, students all across the country are benefiting from her insight.

YOU ARE NOT YOUR CHILD'S FRIEND

Most parents are under the assumption that you can be both a parent and a friend to your child. Nothing can be further from the truth. You are a parent **first**. It is not until your child grows older that you can bridge the gap between parent and friend. When your child is young, you want to teach them values, morals, structure and discipline. What you don't want to happen is your child become confused about the hierarchy of the relationship role between parent and child. In other words, you don't

Did You Do Your Homework? Is Not Enough!

want your child to look at you as just another one of his or her friends. It can lead to major problems.

The relationship between parent and child is consequential. It cannot be compromised. Many parents tend to compromise their relationship with their child in order to be liked by them. That's not your role. Your role is to teach them everything they need to lead successful and productive lives. That means you establish strict discipline, set rules that are clear and consistent, and always remember to keep the levels of communication open.

Keeping the levels of communication open does not mean that your child becomes your best friend. There's a fine line between the way you converse with your friends and the way you converse with your children. Your children are not your peers. They are your dependents, and they depend on you for strength, wisdom, and guidance. Too many times parents rely on their children for companionship. This can cause undo stress and eventually innumerable problems in the long run in relation to other adults.

The core meaning of discipline is "to teach." Children crave discipline. When you develop a social intimacy with your children they will lose respect for you. It changes the relationship and it changes the way your child perceives other adults. Students whose parents have developed a friendship

Did You Do Your Homework? Is Not Enough!

with them are argumentative, readily frustrated, and easily angered. They are the students who think they know everything and they don't take well to direction. This is because they've experience a false sense of adulthood from their parents.

This is not to say that you can not laugh, joke and have a great time with your children. It is a must that you as a parent enjoy your children's unique personalities. However, the roles of your relationship must be clearly and precisely defined. My mother used to say, "Don't get too comfortable that you slip up!" There is a fine line that your children know they must not cross.

Aaron Braxton

I was speaking with a friend on the phone. As we were talking he was telling his two young sons to get ready for church. Every few minutes he would break the conversation to tell his five year old to put on his shoes. After about the fourth time of telling his son to put on his shoes, he gave him a light pat on his behind (this is not a plug for corporal punishment). Of course the five year old started to cry.

Seeing the whole commotion, the two year old started repeatedly saying to his father, "Don't you hit my brother!" His father responded by saying, "Be quiet." The 2 year old's response was, "You be quiet!...Don't you hit my brother!" His father then said, "Shut up!" The two year old then said, "You sh….be quiet…Don't you hit my brother!" Even at two years old he knew where to draw the line. He knew that if he told his dad to "Shut up" there would be dire consequences.

This is not to suggest that children don't occasionally "slip up." Nonetheless, when this happens actions must be addressed and corrected immediately. You can not wait until the second or third offense. You will be sending your child mixed messages which your child will definitely question. This means you will spend unnecessary time on explanation and your child will gradually begin to lose respect by continuing to question your authority.

DISCIPLINE

When most people think of discipline, they think of constant yelling and screaming. Some think of various degrees of punishments. While still others think of only the "belt."

As mentioned earlier, the core meaning of discipline is "to teach." This means teaching your children positive behavior which you'd like to see them demonstrate in their everyday lives. It's about setting limits and boundaries which can never be crossed. It is not about you controlling your

Did You Do Your Homework? Is Not Enough!

children, but about you teaching your them to be self controlled. It's about keeping them safe until they are able to care for themselves in a manner in which they are accustomed. Children who have a secure grasp of self control, are most likely to have an assured and positive self image.

There will be times when your children will test the rules. Instead of immediately "going off" remember your children are doing what they are supposed to do. It's their way of testing you. They want to know from *you* how far *they* can go. It's up to you to confirm that your rules are real and don't need to be tampered with. Also remember that children may need to be told rules several times before they internalize them. This holds especially true for young children. You may want to give a few warnings to remind them of the rules.

When you are reprimanding your children, let them know what behavior is expected of them. Tell them that you know they are capable of following the rules and regulations of the house. Try not to make personal attacks. Only attack the behavior. Kids know when they've done wrong and in many cases they feel bad already. By making personal attacks you don't want your children to automatically become defensive.

When the reprimand is over, it's over. Let them know how much you appreciate when they are on their best behavior and have practiced self control. Give them a hug or a slight touch and move on.

I LOVE YOU

Love is a natural emotion. It is *spiritual* and *unconditional*. It is, moreover, extremely important that children feel they are loved. It is a parent's number one responsibility to let their children experience their love. Therefore, you must say the phrase "I love you" often. Most parents usually say it to their infant children, but when their children reach adolescence they somehow feel it's not a needed expression anymore. It's not enough to think that your children "know" they are loved. It's important to "show" they are loved. That means, *show it*, even when you think your children aren't very appreciative.

Kiss your children often. Outstretch your arms as far as they will go and hug them often. Tell them when they do a terrific job, but first and foremost, tell them you love them with all your heart and back it up with action.

SUPPORT

Children need to feel they are supported. That means taking time out of your schedule to support them. It is essential for them to know that you have a stake in what they are doing. Whether it's a parent conference, a sporting event, or a school spelling bee, children need to feel that you have an invested share in their interest and development. There are too many parents who are absent from their children's developmental lives. Ask any teacher how many parents actually show up for parent conferencing. Most teachers will say approximately 10-25%. What kind of message are you sending to your children and their teacher?

Support your children when they are doing well. Offer them all the positive reinforcement you can muster. This says to them that they are on the right track. Tell your them often that you are proud of them. Let them know how fortunate you feel to be their parent. Whether they've received an "A" on an exam or cleaned the house without prompting, let them know that you champion them and that you'll always be in their corner.

Support also means encouraging your children to try new things and don't be discouraged when they refuse. One day they just love ice skating and the next day it's archery. The day after it's field hockey then it's photography. Whatever it is, encourage them to continue to search for their unique inner skills. Only then will they know what they like and what they dislike. At least they keep narrowing the field down a bit. Even if you have children who don't feel they have any particular interest. Keep

Did You Do Your Homework? Is Not Enough!

searching with them. You may ask the question, "What are some of the things you like to do?" Always remember to get them involved in the activities they enjoy and don't be discourage if that enjoyment fades in a day. At least your children will feel their interest are being supported.

Even the child who is displaying negative behavior can be helped if they feel they are being supported. Address the behavior directly and finds ways to use positive reinforcement rather than a negative one.

THE FEELING OF FREEDOM

Children should feel that they can ask you anything, especially when they are young. Too many parents get frustrated when their children are constantly asking "what, when, why, or how." Instead of responding by saying, "Stop asking me so many d#%n questions!" Be prepared to offer some advice. Next time when you feel like you're going to explode out of pure frustration and stress, try pointing them in directions where they may find answers. Suggest where information of greater depth can be located and what areas of study will be helpful.

Did You Do Your Homework? Is Not Enough!

There are many reference materials that may be useful. You might invest in encyclopedias, a computer, or simply take them to the library. My mother made the commitment in my early development by investing in encyclopedias: therefore when I had an unequivocal question, I simply remember her saying, "Look it up." That saved her a lot of frustrations, but it also gave me a sense of my own independence. I felt very grown up and empowered when I researched things on my own.

DON'T LET THE <u>SMALL</u> <u>STUFF</u> GET YA!

Too many times parents want to correct every small idiosyncrasy their children possess. Some things can be left alone or simply corrected with a simple reminder. Unless it's harmful to themselves or others, it's sometimes best to leave it alone. In many cases whatever the idiosyncrasy, it will go away with time, without the constant nit picking.

SMALL STEPS FIRST

There's an old saying, "You must crawl before you walk." That is such a true statement. So many children feel that changing is such an enormous process. The reason is because they visualize the beginning process, all the stuff in the middle, and the end results. What they don't tend to realize is that "successful end results" begin with "enthusiastic small steps."

VICTOR

Victor was a former student who always found himself in the office because he could not control his behavior. He wasn't a malicious child. He was a child who could not control his constant annoying talking. When he was confronted with his behavior he was often rude and obnoxious. It was for this reason he was regularly sent to the counseling office.

One day I sat next to Victor while he was waiting to be seen by his counselor. I asked him if he enjoyed being regularly sent to the office. His response was, "No!" My next question then became, "Why do you continually do things that will get you into trouble?" His response was the same response every middle school child gives, "I don't know." I asked him if he wanted to change and his reply was, "Yes, but it's hard!"

Of course change is hard if you've been used to doing things a certain way and all of a sudden you're confronted with change. It's even harder if you start to view the situation as one enormous procedure. It can even be very overwhelming. My

Did You Do Your Homework? Is Not Enough!

grandmother always said, "Do what you can today, and tomorrow will take care of itself." I always tell my students to concentrate on the process at hand. It is not a good idea to get too far ahead of yourself. Then the task at hand becomes too large. However, if it is broken down into smaller steps (which can also be classified as goals) the process becomes much easier to handle.

In the case of Victor, I told him to concentrate on his behavior on an hourly basis. It was impossible for him to perceive himself abruptly changing all at once. He could not commit to being good for the entire school year, but he could commit to being good for a half an hour. After that half an hour was over he could commit to another half. Then he could go from a half an hour to an hour. Then from an hour to a half a day. Then from a half a day to a day. Eventually we'd want to get him to commit to an entire school year. However, had we started with committing to an entire school year, it would never have worked. He would have felt astounded.

Victor knew that somewhere in the near future he was going to "screw up." Knowing this, he did not want to put that kind of pressure on himself. Therefore, he just constantly acted inappropriately. When he was informed that his behavior could change *gradually*, he was more inclined to accept

Did You Do Your Homework? Is Not Enough!

this gradual process. The pressure was then off of him to change drastically all at one time.

Even as adults we sometimes look at the enormity of situations. If we can take the time to stop and rethink about things from a child's prospective, we will get a clear understanding of how *small steps* really helped us to prosper. Remember that old saying, "You must crawl before you walk." Whether it's working on math concepts or teaching your child how to clean the bathroom remember to break things down into small steps so that they will not get overwhelmed with the bigger picture.

5

IMAGINATION

IMAGINATION

Imagination is a fundamental skill that must be developed during childhood. It is a very important process in the development of the *creative mind* from childhood to adulthood. If the process of developing a child's imagination is somehow neglected, it can have detrimental effects on the

Did You Do Your Homework? Is Not Enough!

maturation of your child's creative processing skills later in life.

Have you ever heard the phrase, "Dare to dream"? Well, if children are lacking an imagination they will, "Dare *not* to dream." The sad reality is that they won't even know how. They will essentially become like the walking dead, living their lives from day to day, just existing.

How do you develop an imagination within your child? You can start by limiting your children's access to video games and television sets when they are young. The unfortunate fact is that although technology is continuing to advance, there are some biting consequences.

The consequences are that children would rather spend long hours becoming virtually brain dead than developing their minds. Have you ever watched a child play video games? It's literally like watching a robot. They are stone faced. The only body part that appears to be alive are their thumbs, which are moving the video game controls. Visual technology such as video games, takes the creative process out of the minds of your children.

There are many childhood games lost today that served a vital purpose when children are young. Remember singing the song "Twenty-nine Bottles of Beer on the Wall?" The song was not only fun, but it served the purpose of learning to add and

Did You Do Your Homework? Is Not Enough!

subtract. How about the game where you had to think of a word for every letter in the alphabet? The winner would think of the next subject such as "Cities." Everyone would take turns thinking of different cities that began with the letter that landed on them. If you couldn't think of a city you were "out."

These types of games were not only enjoyable, but they developed the creative mind as well.

THE CREATIVE MIND

What is the creative mind and how do you develop it? The creative mind is that part of yourself that controls imagination and mental images. It allows one to dream, visualize, and fantasize. It can be vast as the universe or as focused as a telescope. When it is developed properly and positively it can create children who dare to become anything their mind perceives.

An ideal way to develop the creative mind is to read to your child. Reading creates feelings and images from words. It allows them to imagine what proper reading sounds like and it gets them excited about the entire process. When parents put the time and energy into reading aloud to their children, they unlock their creative minds. They unlock the mysteries of the universe. Children can visit Mars, Africa, California, or the imaginary cities of *Narnia*

Did You Do Your Homework? Is Not Enough!

or *Dune*. They can read about kids "morphing" into other animals in order to protect the world or be scared for life by creepy crawlers. All and all reading aloud develops a vast imagination and gets to the root of the creative process.

Another ideal way to develop the creative mind is to teach reading through drama. Many families do this spontaneously by acting things out. Whether it is having weekly talent shows or memorizing Easter speeches, families find ways to unwittingly create drama. The next level would naturally be to bring the same excitement and play to literature. This can be attained from fairy tales, folk tales, and even comic books. Literature provides excellent material for creating the creative mind within your children.

MENTAL PICTURES

Mental pictures are images your child creates in his or her mind while learning is taking place. These images are formed from some type of stimulus, whether that be reading aloud or giving directions. Children must be able to create these images in their head first, before they can be retained later.

There are some students that tend to do well when given oral directions and others that have to have directions repeated several times. At first I wondered why this took place. Then I started to realize that the students who tended to grasp concepts from the start were the same students who tended to have an imaginary mind. These students were able to grasp concepts from the start because they could make mental pictures in their heads regarding directions.

It's the same concept as joke telling. Those people that get jokes the first time are the people who have the ability to create mental pictures of the jokes while they are being told. While those whose imagination aren't quite as developed tend to miss jokes and have to have them repeated several times before they "get it."

Children are the same way. Those that have not had the opportunity to fully develop their imaginary minds tend not to "get it" the first or even the second time. Things often have to be repeated because they are not able to create the mental pictures needed to sustain an interest in a teacher or parent's conversation. These students are inclined to get lost and when they are questioned, their immediate response is, "I don't know."

SILENCE

Children must become aware that they possess an inner voice. The only way this can happen is

Did You Do Your Homework? Is Not Enough!

through *silence*. It is through this silence that children will begin to actualize who they really are.

In many instances it is very difficult getting children to be quiet even for a moment. Most parents will think, "Yeah right, I can't get them to be quiet even when they're asleep!" But you must remember that *silence* can be a prayer at the dinner table. It can be a silent moment when your child goes to bed. It can be a silent moment when you leave the house in the morning. It doesn't have to be for hours. It may only last for a few minutes. However, it is important that your child have a silent moment every day so that they begin to not only hear their inner voice, but trust in it as well.

THE SUBLIMINAL

A baby recognizes its' mother's voice while still in the womb. A patient still hears the encouraging words of family members while in a coma. How can this be possible? It is possible because even when we are in an altered state there is the potential for brain activity to take place, and for us to listen.

Take the time to quietly talk with your children while they are sleeping. Tell them how *creative, intelligent, beautiful, loved*, and *wanted* they are. Let them know that they are already leaders and that there are no limits to their success. Within their

Did You Do Your Homework? Is Not Enough!

sleep give them a sense of comfort and peace. Even as they are dreaming, they will hear you.

PROBLEM SOLVING

If you want your child to be proficient in all areas of life, take the time to develop his or her creative imaginary mind. It will also improve their range for *problem solving*.

Most people can not adequately problem solve because they do not have an adequate imagination. Problem solving takes imagination and creativity. One must be able to see all possibilities and act on them.

People who do not have an adequate imagination cannot problem solve and only see one situation at a time. They react to problem situations out of fear. It's like seeing a glass half full or half empty. If one views the glass as half full, then one imagines all possibilities. If one views the glass as half empty, then one can imagine *only* the situation at hand.

Problem solvers react to situations out of pure potential. They ask themselves the question, "What can I learn from this?" Challenges become events. One is able to clear obstacles like a world class hurdler competing in the Olympic final of the 110 meter hurdle event.

Did You Do Your Homework? Is Not Enough!

Having the ability to imagine several possibilities opens one mind to limitless prospects. If a situation doesn't work, then one is able to think clearly of something else. One is not restrained, but free. One doesn't look at the world or it's situations as disjointed pieces of a puzzle. It is this ability that allows one to think of the world as a beautiful puzzle with pieces to decipher. This permits ones' world view to be totally open. Life is not a complete mystery with clenched fist and closed doors. Life is a continuous wonderment with endless possibilities and boundless opportunities.

6

What *You* <u>Owe</u>

<u>What You Owe</u>

Children are not asked to be brought into this world. It is one of the only things they don't have complete control over. The choice was made for them, by you, the parent. As their parent, you *owe* them everything you can do for them from the very first moment of their conception.

Did You Do Your Homework? Is Not Enough!

Some parents might have a hard time with the concept of *owe*. They feel that by saying the word *owe*, it brings about with it *expectations* and *obligations*. These parents don't want to feel obligated to their children, nor do they want their children to expect too much. This takes the pressure off them as parents.

It is the right of your child to expect the very best in you. It is only then can they expect the very best in themselves. Words are symbols. They mean something. By saying that you *owe* your child, you are saying that you want to give your child the very best out of life.

Wanting the very best for your child doesn't mean that if your child graduated from high school that you go into debt buying him a Porsche. It also doesn't mean that your child comes to you with a long list of demands. It simply means that you, as the parent, pledge to make a conscious commitment to the well being of your family.

Words are symbols. They mean something to the conscience mind. Consequently you want to put into your mind the strongest symbols possible when it deals with the future of your children. The word *owe* is a strong symbol. It means there's an unpaid balance that you as the parent owe your child for bringing him or her into existence. It's a balance

Did You Do Your Homework? Is Not Enough!

that's always outstanding, and sometimes even overdrawn. But you continue to graciously pay it knowing that the positive effect is the greatest reward.

BUILDING SELF- ESTEEM

Most children have a saying, "Sticks and stones will break my bones, but words will never hurt me." I wish that were true, but unfortunately it is the furthest from the truth. Words are very powerful and often times can cause drastic emotional injury to a child's fragile self esteem. It is for this reason parents have an obligation to choose words and phrases that will be beneficial to the healthy development of their child's blossoming self image.

Most parents would not intentionally degrade their children. In spite of that, even asking questions like; "What's wrong with you?" "Are you out of your mind?" or "Why are you making a mountain out of a mole hill?" can be emotionally damaging and cause grave psychological injury to a child's self esteem.

Along those same lines, phrases such as: "You are driving me crazy!" "You are getting on my last nerve," "I'm about to knock you into the middle of next week," or even "You make me sick!" are also emotionally damaging and must be avoided at all cost. Building a child's self esteem means never being insulting, swearing, or calling them any derogatory names.

Keep in mind that damaging a child's self esteem takes years of aggression, so don't beat yourself up for the occasional slip up. Just remember that words do hurt and that caution and caring are necessary in order to bring up self assured individuals.

TIME

Time is very valuable. It is one of our greatest commodities. Unfortunately many children take it for granted. As adults we begin to realize that time is important, and that it must be cherished. This is an idea that needs to be passed down to your children.

We don't know how long we have on this earth, therefore we must make every second count towards something. While we are on this planet, every step we make should be one toward achieving our specific goals. This concept is one that ought to be taught to children.

Children must be made aware that they are not invulnerable. There are factors in their lives that they have no control over. Consequently, they must make every effort to make every single one of their actions count. They are going to slip and they are going to forget, but it is up to you to remind them

Did You Do Your Homework? Is Not Enough!

constructively that every one of their actions counts towards their future and the betterment of their lives.

Many times parents come home from their busy schedules and they are too tired to spend time with their children. Remember, your children did not ask to come into this world, therefore it is your responsibility to muster up the energy in order to spend *time* with them, nurture them, and in many cases, answer questions that may be "over their heads."

Time is also about making a conscious effort to be at every one of your child's parent conferences. There may be important engagements that arise, but you must ask yourself the question, "Is the time I spend somewhere else important enough for me to miss the progress report of my child?" In many cases the honest answer will be "No."

Another factor where time is imperative is in the morning. You owe it to your child to make sure that they have a complete breakfast in the morning. It is necessary for their health, development, and over all well being that they have a hearty meal in the morning before school. I have seen many parents leave the responsibility of breakfast up to the school system. Please take note that these are the same systems that classify ketchup as a food group. Because breakfast is the most important meal of the

Did You Do Your Homework? Is Not Enough!

day, it is doubly important that *you*, as their parent, be there for them during this crucial time.

SOCIAL EVENTS

It is eminently important that you attend your child's social events. Whether they are in a kindergarten play, a school parent/teacher conference, or a high school track meet, you must make your child feel supported. It is part of the unpaid balance you owe your child.

I remember when I ran track and field in high school. One of my favorite events was the 300 low hurdles. The hardest thing about that specific race was that you started on one side of the track and you finished on the opposite end. What was particularly grueling was there were 30 inch hurdles you had to clear as well.

As I would round the curve toward the finish line in any given track meet, I used to be able to drown out all the other sounds of the meet: crowds, announcers, even other athletes; and concentrate on my mother's *voice* in the stands. When I reminisce with friends over my days of glory, it amazes them that I could hear my mother shouting, "Go, Aaron!" over the sometimes thousands of people in any stadium. "How could you drown all those people out?," said my friends. "Because I *wanted* to," I said.

Did You Do Your Homework? Is Not Enough!

It was important for me to hear my mother and concentrate on her voice in my head. It made me feel stronger and run faster. It made me believe I could win, and in 90 percent of my races, I did (I became the league champion and went on to compete at the California State Track and Field Meet in three different events).

Sometimes, it even amazes me at how connected I was. Yet, I know it was all purposeful. My mother's voice extended beyond the track and field. It extended throughout my life. Her sincerity in my social events made me trust that she had my best interest at heart. Because she made me important, I felt important, and I wasn't going to do anything to jeopardize her faith and support.

VACATIONS-nature

Vacations leave lasting impressions on children. Often they are remembered for a lifetime. Take at least one family vacation a year. Preferable one that involves the outdoors. When children are outdoors nature's delicate balance has a serene effect on them. Why do you think most children like summer camp?

Being one with nature has such an important positive effect on children. It is for this very reason most schools have overnight camps set up for "at risk" children during the school year. Once these troubled children return back to school, most have changed their impertinent behavior. This is because nature and all it's enduring principles leaves a positive impression about the structure of life.

Nature reminds us that we are all connected. It's an infinite structure that's always changing, always growing, but never ceasing to discard any of it's parts. Nature constantly replenishes itself while continuously regenerating itself.

As a parent, you must allow your children to experience these phenomenons first hand. Only then will they begin to see that they have a place in this beautiful cycle we call life.

RELIGION

When children are young it is vital that they receive some type of spirituality. In today's day and age, children have to be taught that there's a greater force out there than they are. They already know that as the parent, you are greater, but they need to know that there's someone greater than you.

As a child my mother forced me to go to church. At the time I never understood why I was learning the things I was learning. All I understood was that it was a task to get up early every Sunday in order to meet my grandmother at 8:00 am.

Every day of the week I had a thriving paper route, and anybody who's ever had a paper route

Did You Do Your Homework? Is Not Enough!

knows that Sundays are the busiest and most strenuous days for paper boys. I was already getting up at 5:00 A.M. every weekday, and now I was forced to get up at 4:00 A.M. in order to finish the route, eat breakfast, shower, and get dressed in time for my grandmother to pick me up for church. I wasn't having it! I tried everything from delivering my papers late, to faking sick. However, my savvy mother would get me up earlier (or later, which didn't make my customers too happy) or simply make me deliver my papers regardless of how I said I felt.

At the time it really bothered me to be forced to attend church services. In spite of that, as I soon relaxed and realized there was no way I could win, I began to enjoy the biblical stories. My mother then relaxed and only required my sister and I to attend Sunday school. That worked for me! To my surprise, I even started to enjoy it.

Now that I'm older I understand what my mother was trying to accomplish. Bible stories are filled with allegories and moralizing stories. These interesting stories are what kept me safe growing up in the inner city of Boston. There were many situations that I could have found myself involved in since my mother went to college at night. However, the metaphoric stories seeped into my subconscious. These subliminal messages kept me

Did You Do Your Homework? Is Not Enough!

from doing things that I was taught to be wrong. The great thing is that, that spirituality continues to this day.

MONEY

Teach your children the importance of money. Tell them about certificate of deposits, the stock market, mutual funds, savings bonds, real estate, ect. If these are areas in which you are unfamiliar, learn about them so you can teach your children. I always tell my students as well as parents, "Books are inexpensive and the libraries are free."

It's imperative that children have a proper respect for money and it's worth. Some people may say that money isn't everything and it won't make you happy. A very wise man once said, "Those people that say that money isn't everything and it won't make you happy, sure never had any!"

Money is power. It is imperative that you consider it in this manner. It may not make you happy, but it will sure make things a lot easier. It does a lot for the comforts of life and children need to understand that it's a necessity in order to function properly in this society. It must be saved, invested, spent wisely and diligently.

An effective way of building a proper respect for money in your children is by giving them an allowance and starting them out with their own

Did You Do Your Homework? Is Not Enough!

savings account. In this way they will begin to understand the importance of saving for things that they need or want. It also works well with the idea of patience and self reliance. It's going to take a long time to buy sneakers that cost $125.00 if they're only putting away $5.00 a week from their allowance into a savings account. Yet, once they reach that $125.00 goal, they will have a better respect and appreciation for budgeting, as well as the concept of paying for what they want on their own. They also won't have you pulling out your hair because they lost those $125.00 sneakers somewhere at school. You better believe, if they bought them, they're going to take care of them.

Because then it becomes *their* hard earned money and not *yours*.

As a parent, you are your child's number one example regarding money. Therefore make sure the examples you show your child are beneficial. This means that your own finances are in tact. Don't let your telephone get cut off. Don't have your child studying by candlelight because your lights were turned off. Don't make your child wear his winter coat to bed because you forgot to pay the gas bill. And by all means, don't let your child go to bed hungry because there was no money in the budget for food.

Did You Do Your Homework? Is Not Enough!

Be a leader and lead by example. That means if your finances are not in order, begin to take the steps to put them in order. It may not be easy and it's not going to happen over night, but it can be done. But, you must make a commitment to yourself and your child and take the step toward a better financial future.

If your finances are in order, then make your child aware of the process and never think they are too young to understand. They will grasp what they can and as you continue the process, so will the process continue in them.

CREDIT

Credit is another area which must be discussed with your children *especially* once they are ready to go off to college. The credit card companies prey on college students and if those students don't have a head for credit they will leave college owing more than just school loans.

Credit is an important asset in society. Not only can it be used to buy assets that will point you and your family in a direction toward financial independence, it can also be used to buy a home, as well as many other needed goods and services. There may also be emergencies that arise where

Did You Do Your Homework? Is Not Enough!

credit becomes an important factor. Therefore it must be protected and taken seriously.

CHARITY

Find opportunities where your family can be of community service. Whether it's beautifying your neighborhood or volunteering at a homeless shelter, find the opportunities to give back the blessings that are bestowed upon you and your family. Charitable contributions are not only meaningful, but can be satisfying, as well as rewarding to everyone involved.

Charity also rears unselfishness in children. People who are unselfish have an increased fulfillment of life because they are making others happy. These types of people realize that what they do has a greater effect on everyone around them. It's a karmic experience in which everyone achieves a, "Win-win" situation.

We as human beings have to be consciously aware of the choices we are making. If you want success in your life, you have to give success to your children. If you want happiness in your life you have to give happiness to others.

When I was a child my grandmother used to repeat the Christian principle, "Do unto others as you would have them do unto you." It is such a profound principle. Whatever it is that you want out

Did You Do Your Homework? Is Not Enough!

of life, you have to give. So, if you want to live large, then you have to give large. It's the law of the universe and it works! The important thing is to be humble to the process and to point out when it is being applied to your children.

7

The

JOURNEY

THE JOURNEY

Children are a blessing. They are a gift that must be cherished, nurtured and held in the very highest reverence. Whether they were created from the purest of love, an accident, or a mistake, children deserve a passionate commitment from the two

Did You Do Your Homework? Is Not Enough!

people that brought them into this world. It is up to those two people to make the choice to enjoy the journey of raising children responsibly. No matter how crazy life gets, and it will get pretty crazy, you must always put the interest of your children first and foremost.

Respond to your children where they are. Not where you are. Many times things may not be going right in your life, but it's imperative that you recognize the beauty within your children. This in and of itself will set off endorphins in your body that will make you feel better. You just have to be open and ready to receive the beauty of the life that you created. It is not that you will forget about your personal problems, but it will make them seem small when you are taking pleasure in the personal lives of your family.

"You reap what you sow" is an interesting statement because it says that you benefit from whatever energy you put into something. Take the case of your children. You as a parent will "reap" whatever you put into the raising of your children. If you want this miraculous experience to be positive, then you must be positive in your demeanor. The rewarding part of this journey is your children will grow into responsible, mature, free thinking individuals. They will have the ability to speak their own minds, listen to their own thoughts, and be

Did You Do Your Homework? Is Not Enough!

their own persons. The beauty is, they will have learned to do this all on their own terms, they will have learned it from you, and they will pass it on to their own children.

As a parent take the time to watch them when they are not being self conscious. Listen to their laughter. Marvel at the life that you've created. Stand in total awe at the sheer magnificence of your own lineage. Always remember that the journey, is part of the process to your total afterglow as a parent. Revel in the time. Cherish the moments. Relax and trust that all is well and continuously taken care of.

HUMOR

Life can get very heavy at times and things can seem so grim. It is at these times that you must take moments to find the humor in life with your children. This will help your children to understand that things aren't always as bad as they seem. And even if they are, there are ways that you can make yourself feel better.

It is said that it takes less muscles in your face to smile than it does to frown. Life brings us so many humorous situations. Smile often, laugh more, and find ways to enjoy life's moments. Let humor inspire you, then pass that torch to your children, so it will inspire them. It's part of the journey.

MISTAKES

Mistakes are wonderful opportunities to learn that which is not known. Once a mistake has been committed, take the opportunity to figure out what went wrong. Try and learn from the mistake so that it is not repeated. It is said that, "Only a fool does something over and over again expecting different results."

As a parent, you don't want to be that person doing the same parenting mistakes over and over expecting to get different results. If something is not working, make a bold move to change and try something new. The task is to enjoy the process of learning from your mistakes. Not only will you begin on the path to reaching complete fulfillment, but your level of comprehension will be much deeper and fear won't even enter into the equation.

Teach your child to ask the questions; What can I learn from this? How can I make this experience useful in my life? When your child is able to *think about*, and *answer* these questions, he or she will be actually experiencing an opportunity to learn.

Possessing the ability to ask yourself these questions also takes the fear out of feeling like a failure if you make a mistake. In this manner failures are opportunities for growth and acceptance. They are learning experiences in which

Did You Do Your Homework? Is Not Enough!

you make the *choice* to become a better person. You take hold of the reins and you control your emotions. You may not be able to control all of your experiences, but you can control your reactions to those experiences. If you react in a positive manner, then you'll get a positive result. If you choose to react negatively, you will bring about a negative result.

Being able to control your reactions is a gift you must give to your children. They need to know that they will make mistakes and that it is a natural progression to learning. If they learn this, they will not only be ready to take on school, careers, and relationships, but life as well.

Aaron Braxton

PEACE

Peace is an altruistic concept that has been taught throughout the ages. It has proven to produce miraculous results when it is applied to the lives of people. It is an idea that must also be instilled in children while they are young.

We as a community must teach our younger generations to become Ambassadors of Peace. It is urgent that they learn to resolve conflicts peacefully and purposefully. We must not allow hostilities to be settled violently and with malice. It causes disharmony.

Did You Do Your Homework? Is Not Enough!

At all times your household, as well as the greater community, needs to be a place of control and harmony. This can only be conducted if *peace* is involved. It moreover, is a belief that begins at home.

Accept the journey as a life long blessing with your children. Love them and know that all is well. Teach them to love themselves and respect others. Guide them in directions that will be beneficial to their existence. Walk with them through the paths of humanity. Carry them through the awkward roads of despair. Above all else, trust and never doubt, that

Aaron Braxton

every need that is in the best interest of you and your children, are already met.

Index

Aaron, 132
Building Self Esteem, 125, 127
Charity, 145, 147
Credit, 144, 145
Discipline, 92, 94
Don and Paxton Miller, 73, 74, 75, 77
Don't Let The Small Stuff Get Ya!, 101
Eduardo, 53, 55
Find A Comfortable Place, 4, 7
Headings, 33, 34
Humor, 152, 153
I Love You, 95, 96
Leadership Amongst Siblings, 56, 61
Mental Pictures, 114, 116
Mistakes, 153, 155
Money, 139, 140, 143
Mychael and Amber, 63, 68

Narrating, 39, 42
Organization, 16, 17, 22
Peace, 156, 157
Problem Solving, 119, 121
Questioning, 34, 37
Reading Introductions, 32
Rebellion, 60, 61
Regina, 80, 85
Releasing Fear, 50, 55
Religion, 136, 139
Reviewing, 41, 44
Silence, 116, 117
Silent Reading, 37, 38
Small Steps First, 102
Social Events, 131, 133
Support, 96, 97, 98
Taneisha and Avery Jackson, 69, 73
The Creative Mind, 111, 113

The Feeling of
 Freedom, 99,
 101
The Process of
 Studying, 28, 31
The Subliminal, 117,
 118
The <u>You</u> in <u>Them</u>, 80,
 85
Time, 127, 129, 131

Time Management, 22,
 27
Turn Off All Music,
 13, 16
Turn Off The
 Television, 8, 9
Vacations, 134, 135
Victor, 103, 105, 106
You're Not Your
 Child's Friend,
 86, 91

About the Author

Aaron Braxton is a true renaissance man. He is a teacher, writer, lecturer, actor, and singer who hails from Boston, Massachusetts. A graduate of San Diego University, he is the author of several inspirational children's plays which have been performed throughout the country.

As an award winning teacher, Aaron has worked as a Resource Specialist in the Special Education Department, where he taught low achieving students using various methods in order to assist them in bypassing departmentalized blocks to learning. He has also developed specialized instructional programs in order to improve student achievement. In addition, he has served as a Drama Department Chairperson where he provided new approaches, as well as a substantial review of all aspects of the performing arts. He has also developed many interdisciplinary workshops with colleagues on various methods to using the performing arts as tool across the education curriculum.

When not in the classroom, Aaron has also worked as a consultant/facilitator for Job Corp., Stop-Gap, Crittiton House, Anaheim Teen Job Training Corp., AT&T, Los Angeles Unified School District, and the Reid High School Teen Pregnancy Program, on such issues as; drugs, teen pregnancy,

AIDS, prejudice, illiteracy, job training, alcoholism, racism, family crisis, rape, goal setting, and education.

Aaron is also a highly gifted actor and singer who has *starred, guest starred,* or *co-starred* in several feature films, television programs, and touring theatre companies.

By always teaching form an artist perspective, Aaron enlightens and empowers his students by offering them the opportunity to think for themselves. When students leave him they are able to challenge information, and view the world on their own terms and from their particular perspectives. He has been praised by parents, peers, and students for his compassion, dedication and hard work.